Negotiating Shadows

Other works by Grace Growing Medicine E.R.

Needs

Negotiating Dramatic Events: Conflict Resolution for Addicted At-Risk Youths in Juvenile Justice

The Fire of Street Joan: A Documentary

The Sami Connection: Journey to North Norway

Grabbing the Gravel in Fairbanks, Alaska

The Making of an Eagle

www.negotiatingshadows.com

Negotiating Shadows

by

Grace Growing Medicine E.R.

GR

George Ronald
Oxford

George Ronald, *Publisher*
Oxford
www.grbooks.com

© Grace Growing Medicine E.R. 2012
All Rights Reserved

*A catalogue record for this book is available
from the British Library*

ISBN 978-0-85398-560-0

Cover design: Steiner Graphics

Contents

To Ester VanKanel and Albert A. Johnson/Dolan
who did the best they could with what they had.
They didn't have much.
The world they were born into
was in a deep shadow of poverty and
chaos, caught between two World Wars.
They did not know how to make it better.
They do now.

Thanks for the help, mom and dad, and to my daughter Jeannie, who endured my shadows as she was negotiating hers.

I dedicate this book to all who are negotiating their shadows – all the drunks, the foster kids, the lonely, the forgotten elderly, the homeless who know they are 'Children of the Other Shoe' but remain hopeful for acceptance anyway, and especially for those who lost the battle and left their shadows behind. They are freer than you or I, my friend!

I want to thank Alcoholics Anonymous for saving my life. Thanks Patty McN and all the other sponsors and 'sponsees' who put up with me as I negotiated my killer shadows on the way to the Sunlight of the Spirit. Finally, to those who don't have to negotiate the kind of shadows talked about in this book, I pray you open your hearts and minds and help change the broken systems that produce Shadow Children.

Introduction

Every day I wake up.
Every day I try.
Every day I wake up. Every day I cry.
I'm a shadow for the Sun.
I'm a shadow
for the Sun.

Poverty. Children of poverty suffer the most. Poverty is still with us. Why? We follow the author's life from a young girl into her womanhood, through her dark journey as she negotiates her extreme life conflicts on the way to her spiritual awakening.

Each chapter opens with a brief note on the history and social conditions of the day, starting in the 1900s and ending in 2011. As we follow her life as it unfolds, we are reminded that the journey to the Sun is difficult, mysterious, miraculous, yet possible and full of wonder. May we all find our spiritual awakening as we dance our Shadows. (I capitalize Shadow several times to emphasize how powerful and personal conflict is, given the right circumstances.) The poetry, embedded after portrayed events, deepens the understanding of the journey.

Statistics 2011

The purpose of this book is twofold: to educate and inform the general public as to the nature of poverty and alcohol/drug addiction and to challenge readers to find their own solutions to the conflict and impact of alcoholism/drugs and poverty on their own communities. Drug/alcohol addiction is a worldwide problem, especially in the US. We are losing youth to addiction phenomena daily. Addressed throughout this book, poverty, and its ripple effect, is profiled through the eyes of an addict who ran the gauntlet, survived near death and is giving back to the community.

[US] National Survey on Drug Use and Health[1]
Substance Abuse and Mental Health Services Administration (SAMHSA)

In the United States in 2010:

- 22.7 per cent of pregnant mothers aged 15 to 17 smoked cigarettes.
- 57 per cent of young adult women aged 18 to 25 drank alcohol.
- 10.8 per cent of pregnant women aged 15 to 44 drank alcohol.
- 16.2 per cent of pregnant women aged 15 to 17 took illicit drugs.
- Approximately 5.4 million adults were on probation and 1.5 million adults were on parole.

- 29.9 per cent of the probationers and 27 per cent of the parolees were current illicit drug users
- The most commonly used illicit drug, with 17.4 million users, was marijuana.
- 51 per cent of people over the age of 12, 131.3 million, were currently drinkers of alcohol.

The DAWN [Drug Abuse Warning Network] Report[2]

In the United States in 2009:
- An estimated 199,000+ alcohol-related emergency department visits were made by patients aged 12 to 20: 76,918 visits for those aged 12 to 17, and 120,853 for those aged 18 to 20.
- 70 per cent of these visits were for alcohol use only, 30 per cent for a combination of drugs and alcohol.[3]

The TEDS Report[4]
Treatment Episodes Data Sets 1999–2009

In the United States in 2009:
- The criminal justice system was the single largest source of referral to substance abuse treatment.
- 42 per cent of admissions to TED were for alcohol, 21 per cent for opiates, 18 per cent for marijuana, 9 per cent for cocaine, 6 per cent for methamphetamines/amphetamines.
- The majority of admissions to TED were males aged between 18 and 44.
- Over a third of probation/parole admissions over the age of 18 had less than a high school education.
- 39 per cent of TED admissions were unemployed.

- The majority of TED admissions had been in treatment at least once; 19 per cent reported they had been admitted three or more times: 43 per cent had not been in treatment before; 12 per cent had been admitted five or more times before.

Excerpts from *The Big Book* of Alcoholics Anonymous

Rarely have we seen a person fail who has thoroughly followed our path. Those who do not recover are people who cannot or will not completely give themselves to the simple program, usually men and women who are constitutionally incapable of being honest with themselves. There are such unfortunates. They are not at fault; they seem to have been born that way. They are naturally incapable of grasping and developing a manner of living which demands rigorous honesty . . .

Our stories disclose . . . what we used to be like, what happened, and what we are like now . . .

Remember that we deal with alcohol – cunning, baffling, powerful! Without help it is too much for us.[5]

AA's Mission Statement

Alcoholics Anonymous is a fellowship of men and women who share their experience, strength and hope with each other that they may solve their common problem and help others to recover from alcoholism. The only requirement for membership is a desire to stop drinking . . . Our primary purpose is to stay sober and help other alcoholics to achieve sobriety.[6]

The Promises

If we are painstaking about this phase of our development, we will be amazed before we are half way through.

We are going to know a new freedom and a new happiness.

We will not regret the past nor wish to shut the door on it.

We will comprehend the word serenity and we will know peace.

No matter how far down the scale we have gone, we will see how our experience can benefit others.

That feeling of uselessness and self-pity will disappear.

We will lose interest in selfish things and gain interest in our fellows.

Self-seeking will slip away.

Our whole attitude and outlook upon life will change . . .

We will intuitively know how to handle situations, which used to baffle us.

We will suddenly realize that God is doing for us what we could not do for ourselves.

Are these extravagant promises? We think not. They are being fulfilled among us – sometimes quickly, sometimes slowly.

They will always materialize if we work for them.[7]

Chapter One

What It Was Like

---

*Between stimulus and
response there is a space. In
that space is our power to
choose our response. In
our response lies our growth
and our freedom.*
Victor E. Frankl

First, the Big Shadow, 1900s
Historical and Social Highlights 1900-39

*Electric cars; disposable blade safety razors; silent films;
Queen Victoria dies; Wright brothers' first flight; Ford
Motor Company incorporated; Titanic sinks; Girl Scouts
of America founded; World War One begins; bread costs
12 cents; Roaring 20s; the Jazz Age; the Charleston; flap-
pers; Prohibition; Al Capone; first radio news programs;
TV becomes commercially available; Wall Street stock
market crash; beginning of the Great Depression; rise of
Adolf Hitler and the Nazi party; Alcoholics Anonymous
born; Amelia Earhart attempts to fly around the world;
World War Two begins.*

When a child is born in a shadow, the child lives in the shadow of its tree. And if its tree lived in the shadow of its trees, then the child is deeply entrenched in the Shadow Dance. The Shadow Dance is one without full sunlight. Sunlight comes in only on shimmering rays, giving the *illusion* there is Sun. Illusions appearing real can lead to paths not easily reversed.

Way before I was born the world system of sane government had broken down. World War One determined my grandparents' path. Then, because sanity is not what governments like to do, the world had to have World War Two. My parents were born into this mess. The Great Depression (imagine calling it Great!) guaranteed insanity on many levels for many people but especially people with no monetary means, no education and in poor health. In the 1920s it was against the law to drink. Prohibition days drove people who had no money into homemade bathtub gin. Our alcoholic ancestors drank in secret and at home. Many died there too.

This was a broken system for marginalized people. *My parents' hearts were broken.* Their basic human needs were not met. They had no way to help themselves, let alone their children. Children have a right to education and support. Without this support, too many children end up on the streets, join gangs, become addicted, are criminals and are lost to society.

Poverty is a barrier to peace. Poverty must be eliminated. Poverty is an enemy of the people. Material deprivation coupled with poverty of spirit kept me from my right to freedom because it kept my parents, my grandparents and my great-grandparents from a place of freedom from poverty. There can be no freedom when poverty and its companions ignorance and fear exist. Feelings of anger, disappointment, sadness, loneliness and worry tear at the very fabric of the spirit of a human being, leading to self-pity, foolish decisions and helplessness. Without unity, oneness, justice and peace. Without these there can be no real human connection. This is a *First Big Shadow*.

They Didn't Have a Prayer, 1940s
Historical and Social Highlights 1940s

World War Two continues, US enters in 1941; US unemployment rate 14.6 per cent (1938), 1.2 per cent (1944); Glen Miller band; gasoline 18 cents; rent $40 month; copper shortage; steel pennies, rationing; concentration camps; Pentagon completed; Janis Joplin, Mick Jagger, Jim Morrison, John Lennon, Paul McCartney born; atomic bombs dropped on Japan; Cold War begins; Marshall Plan for the reconstruction of Europe begins.

My parents came from hardworking farmers, stonemasons and survival type people. On my father's side, a long line of strugglers, losers, alcoholics, thieves – poverty-stricken but tough, resilient people. There were many children (14) living on the river in the mud, in poverty, in ignorance. My father had many dreams. He was off the chart brilliant even though he only made it to the eighth grade. He learned to fix cars, wire houses, repair appliances. He knew stuff. He would give it away for a six-pack of beer, Papst Blue Ribbon, to be precise.

My dad was an alcoholic. He did not know he was an alcoholic. Alcoholics Anonymous was too new in those days. AA made an appearance in 1935 in Akron, Ohio. Dad lived in Ohio at the time. It was as if the very ship that could have saved him passed in the night. As far as I know, he never heard of the great ship called AA. So he worked, drank and danced a poverty dance. Many took advantage of my father.

He loved the racetracks. He gambled and lost most of the time. He had hope. He wanted to be a winner. When he did win at the tracks we ate steak and had many gifts, but most of the time we were dirt poor, cold, hungry and frozen in these times and I was born into the shadow of his shadow. Dad died from cirrhosis of the liver.

On my mother's side there were religious people. We can trace her ancestry back to Switzerland. But they did not stay there. They moved to USA, to Ohio. My grandfather, Noah, was a minister. My grandparents had 14 kids, my mom being one of the youngest. By the time my mom was born, her mom, my grandmother, was worn out and didn't have much to give to my mother. Mom probably had some brain damage, certainly emotional damage.

My mom was smart and pretty and 'man crazy', so they said. My mom had little support except the promise of her people's religion. Her religion failed her. She loved Jesus but He was all she had. Her people were not there when she eventually found herself homeless, living in a car, and alone. She died of cancer.

Her brothers had a good life. They lived in fine houses

and had fine families. They tried to help her but their help came with heavy-handed agendas and conditions. The gulf between them and her prevented anything that could have made a difference. She was condemned by her family as a 'whore'. That's what she had – condemnation and Jesus.

How my parents met, why they thought they should have kids, I don't know. But they did. I remember some of that time together. Mom and dad tried to live together, to be a couple with three kids. He worked hard, she tried to be a mom, but they were steeped in poverty, ignorance and fear. They stayed together at least six years while they negotiated their life path. Her alcoholic drove her crazy and her craziness drove him away.

The Shadow Dance Begins, 1943

Before I was born my dad robbed a liquor store to give my mom some comfort, like food. The police were after him, and when he and my mom crossed county lines, the FBI were involved. My mother was about to have me. They got as far as northern Ohio, where she went into labor. He left her on the doorstep of a hospital.

I was born in Cleveland, Ohio, while my dad was on the run, in June. My last name was Dolan even though my dad's name was Johnson. He changed his name to Dolan, after a famous fighter of the time, to escape the law. The birth certificate is stamped with an Ohio seal in June but my parents celebrated my birthday in July – all my documents are July, the certificate says July even though the seal is June. So July it is. I was a full-term baby who weighed in at five and a half pounds. I was a full-term preemie.

My mom smoked non-stop. My growth was stunted as a result. I was born compromised, long, thin, damaged, and a little fetus criminal, right from the start. This was my shadow birth. The Shadow Dance had begun. There is a world where people have the luxury of dancing with their illusions of safety, justice, plenty and happiness.

There is another world that is all too real for many people on Earth. That one includes suffering, poverty and pain. No illusion there, just reality. These two worlds need to talk with each other.

Their Story

I was their story. I was their music.
They had me at 'Hi my name is' all Willy-Nilly.
This without thought, all action in hot sheets driven
by a hundred forms of sex-driven hormones and
pheromones,

a thousand forms of fears, delusions and illusions

and centuries of DNA manipulation

by the Gods

uttering 'bring forth those that will make mention of me'

They stepped out, ponies out exposed.

Risky business this.

Army or Jail?

My dad was caught and was given the option of going to jail for armed robbery or going into the army. He chose the army. He was shipped overseas and for four years he fought and killed Japanese in the jungles of the Pacific. My mom was alone with a new baby (me) with nowhere to go. My dad's sister Mary took us in. Aunt Mary resented my mom and her ability to have children. Mary was barren. She intimidated my mother, made her feel inferior and, according to society, she was. Mary found an upper middle class man and married well; mother married a thief. Society condemned those who didn't marry well. My mother was under this shadow for three years until my father got back from the war. My father was damaged when he returned. My mother was damaged at birth. The damage continued. Damaged people stay that way until some miracle occurs. Sometimes the miracle does not appear.

Born Story Laden

I was only about four or five years old but I remember parts of my time together with mom and dad. We were living in a small apartment in the back of an old lady's big house in Dayton, Ohio. My parents struggled to pay rent, buy food and raise three kids. I remember the cries of a puppy coming from under our apartment and my dad crawling into a tight hole to rescue it. There was the time when a man at the gate of the yard asked me to come over to him. My mom popped out of the door, grabbed my arm and pulled me back into the house. She tried to protect and watch us.

There was also the time I was walking to school (1st grade?) and a kid by the name of Danny Bird jumped out from behind a tree and stabbed me in the wrist with a small knife. I ran back to the house and dad scooped me up into his arms, rushed to the local doctor's office. I remember how safe I felt in his arms. I remember how worried and angry he was. He found where Danny's parents lived and went to them to see why their kid had stabbed his kid. My mom and dad loved us.

One night we heard fire alarms. The house across the street burned down. A small child was killed in that fire. I remember my mom reading from her Bible and telling us kids how little children go directly to heaven. She prayed that we all go to heaven.

I'm Out Here . . . Part One

I remember my dad saying to me, once during one of his good memory (more sober) days, that when I was born I was so long and thin that my feet stuck out of the baby buggy when he was taking me for a walk in a bad neighborhood of Dayton. He was proud of his little baby. I need to remember that. Well, here I was out of the womb, into Life 101 with all its incoming. Ready for something to happen. Little did I know that all kinds of something were going to happen. What drama, what presentation, what witnessing, what a deal! Well, here I am, world! Let's go! Perhaps I am up for it. Perhaps I can negotiate this Shadow, the one I was born with and into. Perhaps.

Born

Born, somewhere, someplace, somehow.
In some hospital, some bed, or alley, or car.

Born, five to seven pounds, more or less. Meth addicted,
smoked, pickled, punked out.

Wanted or not loved. Coming out weary, angry.
Launched out with or without thought.

You didn't ask me to be born!

Underprivileged, undereducated, underplanned
under a bridge screwing up.

Hard to be human. Required however. Born alone by
some mom born alone, spawned by father born alone.

We die alone.
Excuse me, I was born, so deal!

Dark Deep Shadow Days in Wooster, Ohio, 1947

My parents fought to the point of extreme violence. We
were living in a big white house. My dad came home
one night with two sacks of groceries, and when my
little brother opened the door to let him in, my mother
hit dad over the head with a cast iron skillet. He should
have died. His head was split wide open and there was
blood everywhere. My two brothers, Dan and Bill, and I

witnessed this event. I was frozen in some kind of time warp that still haunts me to this day. My two brothers were traumatized for the rest of their lives. This, my friend, is a deep dark shadow that even the sunlight has a hard time reaching.

After she hit my dad, mom took us kids, ran out into the dark night, through a cemetery, out onto a country road, miles away from our house, and left us on the doorstep of her sister, in the middle of the dark night, out in the middle of nowhere on an Ohio farm, wrapped in a blanket. This was our first foster home. Mom's sister, Bertha, was old, washed out, weary, bitter and disappointed. She was extremely abusive and angry.

This is where my mom and dad chose to leave us kids. I never did find out why. I never did find out if they had options or where they went after the 'dumping of the children ritual' happened or why they never came back for us. I never found out. I do know they struggled for years to make it after dad got back from the war. They tried. I remember some of their conversations. I know my dad worked hard to get small jobs here and there in between bar stops but we never had enough warm clothes, food or heat for the big drafty white house. We would never see that house again.

School Daze

I remember going to school but there are still big chunks of memory gone as to the details of these days. We kids would walk down a long driveway to wait for the school bus. When I got on, I would receive the bully treatment that kids are so good at. The big farm boys would pin me to the window side of the bus and I thought my ribs were going to break. The pain was horrible. I would scream but the bus driver ignored it. One day an older girl, Mary Jarvis, got up, pulled them away and sat me on her lap. She was a big girl and she saved me from those bully boys. I remember grieving when she no longer rode the bus. She graduated from elementary to go on to junior high. One day her family drove all the way out to the country to pick me up so we could go to a school event. Eventually she disappeared from my life. I hope your life is well, Mary. You were my angel.

Robots One and All until Polio Days

Schoolteachers were not trained to interfere with children's lives at home. My teachers taught by rote, as if they were robots. I don't remember connecting with any of them. I do remember the cruel way I was handled when I could not remember my lessons. I was humiliated and punished, only to go home and be humiliated and punished. My escape was to go into a blissful daze and stay there as much as possible. I was grateful for being able to zone out. Out of body was a good thing. I survived the cruel shadow that encased me at this time.

Polio hit our part of the country. I remember the nurses who came to the schools to give us shots. There was one girl who got polio. Her name was Alice Chipner. I was her seatmate until one day she disappeared and it was announced she had polio. I remember riding my bike to her house to visit her. She had to lie on wool blankets and be carried around the house. The thought at the time was that wool blankets helped the polio. The Chipners were poor people. Their house was very old and her parents were poor farm people. She had heavy leg braces. I went to visit her often.

We became friends. She was so brave and I admired her. I was the Sun to her shadow. I did not know at the time how much of a Sun she needed. I remember feeling good when I went to visit her. I remember feeling warm inside. I think Alice's polio changed many of the teachers too. The robots started to connect and talk to us kids. I remember polio was a good teacher to the teachers.

This Mom and Dad

Society was not kind to either one of them. They were children of the Great Depression. The state of 'poverty, poverty everywhere and not a drop of gold to be found to save us' was a reality for people like mom and dad. The rich and wealthy had it all and did not much care for people of my kind. Even today the banks, the wealthy, the rich, the privileged have more advantage than the poor. It needs to change. It is now the year 2011. When will it change?

My mom was born on January 7, 1911 and died on May 12, 1993. She was someone's kid once. She brushed her hair, washed her face, put makeup on, dressed her thin, pretty body with clothes. She went to school and graduated from the Fairview Park nursing program and Boyd Business College. She drove a car, made love, cried, laughed, celebrated holidays, made phone calls, went to the bank, took walks, lifted her children to her breast, took pictures, bragged about her kids and her husband, and fought with them too. She prayed and cursed, she marveled at the flight of the butterfly. She died homeless.

My dad bet on the ponies, bellied up to the bar to brag about the life he had and wanted. He had friends and enemies, he went to war and fought for his country and kin. He loved his dogs and kids and wife. He screwed up on a regular basis. He did the best he could with what he had. He had dreams and desires, most of them never realized. He was a good guy. He died ashamed.

They don't do any of this now. They are dead. It will soon be my turn and yours. We have to consider why we are here. We have to do better, be kinder to one another. We must not leave this world in the same condition that we found it or the way they found it. My task is to honor their suffering. We must do better.

No one asked me whether I wanted to be born. I did not have a choice. Nobody consulted with me about who my parents were going to be. This pissed me off later on. I stayed pissed off for years. This was a big non-negotiable shadow. This shadow drowned me, and kept me, in darkness for many years. Anger and resentment are a big deal in the shadow world. The Shadow Kingdom thrives on the 'dubious luxury' of being angry. These are killer shadows. The Sun missed me, it ached when I was born. An unborn baby should not come into the world pissed off.

Chapter Two

What Happened

*It happens when it
happens and when it
happens it just is and there
is nothing you can do to
undo it.*
Attributed to Buddha

Historical and Social Highlights 1950s

*The Beat Generation; Korean War; Cold War continues;
Apartheid; Mau Mau uprising; McCarthyism; Tibet invaded
by China; Algerian War; bomb shelters; hula hoop craze;
Nikita Khrushchev; President Dwight D. Eisenhower; Suez
crisis; coffee 59 cents lb.; Alaska and Hawaii become states;
school segregation by race declared unconstitutional;
Cuban revolution; Fidel Castro; Kodak Brownie Flash cameras; first copy machine; rock 'n' roll; decolonization of Asia
and Africa begins; Elvis Presley; Marilyn Monroe; European
Common Market established; development of computers;
Sputnik; space race; first plastic Coke bottle; double-helix
structure of DNA identified; Salk and Sabin polio vaccines.*

Isolation, Dislocation and All that Jazz, 1950s

Loneliness is an awful, awesome state to be in, especially for someone so young. A child who is lonely is in a desperate place. It is a horrible world of its own. We humans are not hardwired for isolation. The brain plays games with the body and with its own realm of grey matter. Loneliness over time produces desolation. Then there are two worlds to dance in, two dark and crazy worlds to negotiate, one to the other. Thank God for booze and drugs. Thank the gods for dislocation. The Shadow Dance that had just begun, began.

The farm, chickens, bulls, field and dell. I became friends with the farm animals. They were my only true friends. My two brothers were OK but they were my brothers. Bill I hated and Dan I protected. I talked to the dogs, especially mine (Tiny), to the cats, cows, chickens, horses, squirrels, mice and birds. They nodded their heads and talked back now and again. Tiny became the most hugged dog ever. When I needed warmth I would go out to the barn and stand with my back to an old docile cow (Betsy). She was the one that allowed me to do so. Lying in the hay helped too. It was warm, smelled good, embraced me and hid me from them out there. I loved the earth and her smell. I still do to this day. My animals are still my best friends. I get them. I almost die when one of my animals dies. I owe the animals of the earth much.

Lard Breakfast and Saving Soap

Have you ever had lard on bread with some sugar sprin-kled on top for breakfast? This is what we kids ate for many a breakfast during the time we were with our par-ents and when we were on the farm. In my parents' case it was lack of money for food; in Bertha's case it was pov-erty-consciousness due to the Depression days. There was plenty of good food on the farm – eggs, milk, corn and such – but she was in a pattern of holding onto what was there because she thought it would go away. They were sure of it. These were the people of the Depression. So we ate the way her mind worked. Even the soap was saved. It was put into buckets of lye water to break it down so it could be used to scrub down the floors and steps.

Oh, Those Farm Steps and Other Chores

I was only six years old. My job was to keep the steep muddy farm steps clean with the lye water, gather the eggs, milk one cow – Betsy, the old cow, that was the gentle one – help with hay baling, ride on the back of the plow with the dust clouds forcing their way deep into my lungs, weeding the garden and hiding the pee-wet bed-clothes from Bertha's gaze. Bertha was raised to believe that beating a child with a long thorn-laden rose bush branch would fix whatever problem the child had.

My brother wet the bed every night and I wet the bed sometimes when I was stressed and exhausted. That meant our bed was wet all the time. We had no heat up there in the attic. We were wet and cold, always wet and cold. It was my job to protect my little brother from the beatings. He was just a baby, so young, so weak, and I knew that if she thought I had wet the bed, she would beat me. She would have killed him if he were beaten.

Children were punished for wetting the bed in those days. They were very cruel Shadow days. The beatings were part of my chores. One morning I was taking the wet sheets out to the clothesline. Bertha found me and made me drag the mattress down the steep farm steps. She beat me and pushed me down the stairs. My kidneys were hurt and I was bleeding at the bottom of the stairs. To make sure I got the message, Bertha put two nails into the wall in front of our bed up there in the cold attic with no heat, and crossed two of those special branches onto the nails.

Some kids have posters of their favorite singers or movie stars in that spot on the wall. We had thorny rose bush branches to gaze upon every night lest we forgot. It is what it is. It was what it was. Deep dark Shadows, my friends! Children are still abused today at this writing. May I ask what is the point? Having been there, done that, I have the right to ask this question, don't I? Wasn't beating me enough? Guess not. If only asking the question would take this shadow away forever.

The Woods as My Mother

I ran into the woods in back of the farmhouse every time I could get away, even in the winter. I identified with Cinderella. I too had all kinds of work I had to do to

23

'pull my weight' around the house and in the barn. Aunt Bertha came from the old school, where children were seen, worked hard, were disciplined hard and tolerated. She had lost the only child she had and was deeply damaged as a result.

When I went to the woods, the shadows would follow me to the edge but could not go in. They stayed on the edge of the woods and I was free of shadows for a little while. I sat on the damp earth in the leaves and moss and talked to the birds and the squirrels. They understood and sent me healing. When I was in the woods I could visit my body again. I could breathe. I wanted the woods to swallow me. I did not want to go back to the edge where those shadows would claim me again. The wood was my mother.

There were some good days, too, but they would not balance the deep Shadow days of abuse. One of my best good memories of this time with Bertha is us kids climbing the cherry trees in the spring, picking the cherries and eating until our guts burst. Seems like the watermelon was just as sweet and bountiful. I am sure Aunt Bertha and Uncle Ora did the best they could with what they had. Bertha was very cruel. She was a child abuser. In those days people were not arrested for child abuse. I was able to have a short conversation with Bertha right before I left for the next foster home. I asked her, 'Why?' She just looked at me as if she did not understand why I was asking. That was the last time I saw her.

When Foster Homes Shift, a Glimpse of the Sun

Ohio was a horrible place to be as a child in foster care, especially when the state did not know you were in foster care. I don't know what happened but somehow my parents must have reported their abandonment to the authorities or someone found out because we three kids were liberated from Bertha's place to Aunt Mary's and things got much better – at least at first.

Aunt Mary and Uncle Butch drove from southern Ohio (Springfield) to northern Ohio (Wooster), packed us up, put us into their car, and we three kids and our little dog Tiny were on our way to our second foster home. The deep shadows of abuse retreated for the first time.

In our second foster home things were better. Aunt Mary, my father's sister, loved us. She could never have children but now she had her children after all. I remember good food every day, and warmth. Love was all around us. I got to sit on her lap and I was hugged. I got to wear pretty dresses. I was clean. My teeth, what were left of them, were brushed. Mary and Butch spent a lot of money fixing my teeth. I went to school. Christmas was magical. We had big lit trees with tons of presents, a warm fuzzy house that smelled of eggnog and nutmeg and turkey and pine. It was good to be warm. It was good to be loved.

Aunt Mary to the Rescue on Tecumseh Road, 1950s

Aunt Mary wanted us kids. She had always wanted me from a baby on and she finally got what she wanted, my mother's three kids. My Uncle Butch was kind, loving, patient and tolerant. They were very brave to take us wild kids into their home. They suddenly found themselves with three crazy children who had been terribly damaged. There was love, even though Aunt Mary had a hidden agenda. I will always be grateful for their rescue.

My Aunt Mary was complicated. She loved dogs and gardens and music. She had a wonderful voice. She sang opera in churches. She seemed happy when she sang. I did what I could to help her enjoy her songs. I think she regretted not singing for a career. In those days women of her status were not encouraged to enter that rare world. She suffered from this loss of career and would mention it quite often.

She had been through some tough times as a kid. Her mom, my grandmother Amanda, lived on the river bottom. The 'wrong side of the tracks' had a deep impact on the girls in this family. Amanda had to put her children in an orphanage. She could not provide for them. Her husband did not help either; he was gone most of the time. The orphanages in those days were horrible.

All my dad's sisters, my aunts, married into upper working class situations. They escaped poverty by the act of marriage. That was the strategy and it worked well for all of them. The men they married were great people. I am not sure they were happy men but they were dedicated men, doing what men did in those days. All my uncles were appropriately polite, respectful, generous and kind, at arm's length. My Uncle Butch was the only exception. He actually enjoyed the hugs and pats on his bald head and play. He was like a father to me. Aunt Mary was jealous of our friendship.

Dad appeared suddenly and ended up living with my Aunt Gladys and his brother, my Uncle Bob, who got him a good paying job at the International Harvester factory. Dad would come to visit and we would go next door and visit him. It was a decent arrangement. I got to be physically near my dad but never emotionally. He was fairly remote with me. He spent more time with my two brothers. I did not see my mom at all. I did not know where she was or what she was doing. Nobody else seemed to care either. When they did talk about my mom, it was always negative.

Uncle Butch taught me how to take pictures with his old box camera. He laughed and joked and talked to me. He was asked to paint a room in my Aunt Gladys's house and he asked me to help him. We put on music (Buddy Holly, The Beatles, Pat Boone, Elvis) and painted the walls. He praised my work. I was a good painter of walls. Imagine that. I was good at something. As it turned out, I was good at many things. This was the first time I heard it.

In 1959 my grandmother Amanda died. I did not know her very well. She was losing her memory by the time she started living with Aunt Mary. I remember her sitting on Mary's front porch and talking about 'goin' yander'. She would gaze out into the open space and repeat that phrase over and over. 'Mary, I'm goin' yander.' I remember asking her, 'Grandma, where are you going?' She would look at me just for a short while and look back at whatever she saw, point and say, 'There, yander!' It made her kind of angry to be asked, so I didn't anymore.

My Very First Car, Job and Kidnapping: Driving Ms. Insanity, 1960s
Historical and Social Highlights 1960s

Yuri Gagarin the first man in space; world population hits three billion; Berlin wall constructed; color television; John F. Kennedy; assassination of John Kennedy, Robert Kennedy, Martin Luther King, Jr; Bay of Pigs; Cuban missile crisis; Vietnam War; Peace Corps created; Civil Rights Act 1964; Che Guevara; hippies; flower power; The Beatles; The Rolling Stones; counterculture; pot and LSD; decolonization of Africa; Rhodesia's Unilateral Declaration of Independence; Biafran War; computer mouse; first heart transplant; birth control pill; first computer video game; tape cassette players; Telstar; gas 25 cents a gallon; summer of love; birth of women's liberation movement; voting age lowered to 18 in Britain; first moon landing.

I graduated in 1960 from Greenon High School in Enon, Ohio, at age 16. Even though I was older and had a better foster home, I still hated school. I was not on the popular girl list, so was not included in much of anything. The girls were so mean. I remember going from one class to another in that daze that I had gotten so used to.

When prom time came, I wanted to go and Aunt Mary bought me a really pretty dress. I went to the prom with a cousin. He disappeared as soon as we got to the prom. So I sat at the table by myself. What was new? I was alone most of the time. I don't remember much of my high school experience. I stayed in retreat mode much of the time. Not the most pleasant memory but at least I went.

Aunt Laura and Cousin Evelyn

I graduated, which is a miracle unto itself, considering my background, and now it was time to get a job. I remember Uncle Butch and me going through the newspaper to find something I could do. Meanwhile my dad was working on a car for me to drive. I didn't know what I wanted to do or what I was supposed to do with my life. My brothers were planning on college. It wasn't even suggested I go to college. It was suggested I find a nice man and get married. Finding a nice man was what I wanted to do – but where, when and how does a young lady do that, there on Tecumseh Road, in the suburbs of a place called Enon, I wondered? I thought there was an opportunity to get out of Enon. My Aunt Laura and cousin Evelyn, who lived in a beautiful house in Columbus, started to talk about me moving in with them. Evelyn, a nurse, was starting to investigate nursing school for me. For some reason, the plan fell apart.

Meeting My First Mister

My first job was at Olan Mills Studio where I learned how to be an airbrush artist. I was paid 65 cents an hour. I loved the job. I drove into Springfield, parked in my spot, which was right across the alley from the back of the loading dock of the post office, and flirted with the guys. There were many good-looking guys loading and unloading the mail into mail trucks. I met Fred that way. Fred was a substitute schoolteacher who worked part-time at the PO and was a bit older than I. He was exactly the kind of guy I wanted in my life. I flirted, he bit, and we had several dates. He picked me up, took me to movies and dinners. We talked into the late night. He was sensitive, intelligent, employed, smelled good and I really fell for him, needless to say.

I was too young for him. I remember him coming to the window of the car as Aunt Mary and I were parking in downtown Springfield, saying 'Hi' and asking me if we could talk. It broke my heart. Still searching for mister, I started to hit the bars right after work from then on. It's not that my heart had been spared from breaking before. Disappointment, discouragement and depression were constant companions. The dark Shadows mandated I stay in this arena. The booze helped.

All Grown Up Now and One-Eyed Driving, 1960s

Aunt Mary was going through some hard times. She had a bout of cancer. She lost her precious chow dog. My grandmother was in failing health. Mary was going through the menopause and her mind was very troubled. She became moody, difficult, and she was on many doctor drugs. Aunt Mary, the person who saved my life, started to turn on me. She stopped the hugs, the love, and the connection between us was broken. I lost my mother again.

It was unbearable and I started to hate her. Things went downhill from there. I started to take her drugs.

Valium was wonderful, and added to drinking, it had a special effect. All I knew to do was put a shield between all the fear and disappointment that was about to destroy me. Hate boiled up inside me and became my shield. Shadows love hate and shields.

Seek and –

So young, seeking my way,
seeking for love and excitement,
seeking for me,
searching for my path.
Searching for mister.
Such a dance I do,
seeking God in a bottle

The Kid was Napped

There was a guy, Kenney, who worked with my dad at the factory. He was interested in me but I was not into him. He was very shy. He had to have an operation. I went to visit him in the hospital, and when I came back to my car, the tire was flat. This guy came out of nowhere to help me. After he fixed the flat tire, he pulled a gun on me, told me to get into the car and drove it out of town.

He stopped the car in the middle of a field way out in the country and tied my hands in front of me with duck tape, put a piece over my mouth, put me into the backseat of the car and drove on. He played the duck tape game over and over. I thought he was going to rape and kill me.

Being kidnapped, tied up, threatened, terrified and compromised does that to you. This guy had escaped from prison. He parked on top of a culvert, carried me down under the bridge, duck taped my ankles together, put my hands behind my back, duck taped them and left. I heard my car driving away.

It was dark, cold, and I was terrified he would return to finish the job. I got my hands loose, untied my ankles and ran barefooted to the first farmhouse. When the people opened the door there was a gun in my face but they realized the situation and called the police.

My need to get the hell out of Springfield was urgent. My Aunt Grace, who lived in Florida, saw an opportunity to help me and was on her way to Springfield.

Aunt Grace to the Rescue

Aunt Grace arrived from Florida with her rescue mission. She had run away from the same difficult, noisy family many years before. She needed a housemaid. I did not know she had a hidden agenda. Girls who had just turned sweet 17 wouldn't at that time. There were no cell phones to call gal friends, only escape routes that seemed they would lead to the Sun. I needed power and control, and Aunt Grace seemed to be the way to that end.

Power

The tassel at the end of the bookmark
Is blowing in the wind
The wind is artificially produced by the fan
In the window, its back faces a still hot day
The fan wind reaches my face
Cooling my passions of the day

I have power – as I walk over to the fan
Switch it to off – silencing all tassel movement.

Ft. Lauderdale, Where that Other Sun Shines

Aunt Grace and I did not work out. I hated that she got up every morning, went to work, leaving me alone in the house all day. I was asked to clean, hang out and do some cooking. I was more alone than I'd ever been. No friends, no family – what a setup. I soon found a crowd I could be with, all those guys and gals on the beach. I became a beach chick. The beach and ocean were so wonderful, mysterious, a far cry from Enon and Wooster, Ohio, and foster homes. So there I was on the beach in Ft. Lauderdale, Florida, at age 17 with a body to die for and all those boys and all those lifeguards and no supervision. Oh yeah! The sun shined all the time, the water was warm and refreshing, the sand was kind on my feet and the boys were interested. Very!

Boys, Booze and Pool Parties

I lived on the beach. It was fun walking around in a bikini and looking good. Oakie was a lifeguard for the city of Ft. Lauderdale. I met him when I was walking up to a beached jellyfish, intending to touch it. He came running up to warn me that they still stung. Oakie introduced me to some other lifeguards. I partied wherever there was a party that happened, every night, somewhere.

Bud, one of the lifeguards, saw I was a young naive girl and he became my protector to a certain extent. Bud raced motorcycles at the track. We dated off and on. I dated Dan too. He was a rich guy with a T-Bird and had access to a yacht. I hung out with the group of lifeguards, beach bums and college comers and goers. I was the girl who hung out. Everyone had a hidden reason for wanting to be with me. I was young, sexy, trusting and up for grabs. It was dangerous. This was a dangerous Shadow with teeth.

Black and White at the Cafeteria, Mid-60s

My Aunt Grace and Uncle Bob found me and finally suggested I go to work. I got a job at a cafeteria. The bathrooms were still segregated. White people went to the white bathrooms and black people went to their bathrooms. The cafeteria hired black people who did the cooking and cleaning up in the back rooms. The front of the cafeteria was all white waitresses, food line chefs, waiters and greeters. The blacks handed food through tiny windows to us who served it up front. The white patronage never saw the blacks. The whites were spared, according to the thinking of the time. Everything black and white was segregated. I was from the north and didn't like the situation, so one day I went to the black bathroom and relieved myself of all sorts of resentment towards the good old boys who managed this mess. I was called up to my boss's office to be told by a red-necked, fat, sweaty, smelly man, 'Proper white girls don't mix with the blacks – you're fired!' It was OK with me. I went back to the beach.

Sex: I am Now an At-Risk Kid!

Eventually sex came online and I was in trouble. I was stoned, drunk, lost, scared and needing to go to a clinic for STDs. The nurse was so harsh and punishing. She demanded I go back to Ohio. She asked for my address there. I gave her a fake one. I never went back to the clinic. The antibiotics worked. I cleared up only to go back to unprotected sex with many partners. There wasn't much emphasis on protection at the time. I was never educated about sex and its dangers. It's not that I was a slut. I was looking for love, connection, community, touch, and I did not know how to do that. I was, as usual, on my own.

Where were the adults? I guess you can say they were negotiating their own shadows and running from their own fears. They did not have time for me and my stuff. I was now an at-risk kid, immature, scared, screwed up and finding myself in deep water. One thing I did know about adults: some of them run away from their kids. They leave them on doorsteps in the middle of the night.

Burning Gold Rings, 1962

All the boys, all the parties and all the booze and drugs did me in by the time I was 18 going on 19. Funny how that Shadow creeps up on you. Soon you are diving into a blue pool at a fancy house on the beach with your top off and too soon the other sun, the one in the sky, starts to burn. The sun burned me quickly. Funny how the sun can burn you even though you are engulfed with shadows, yours and others'. I found myself pregnant. Bud, Dan,

Oakie and all the rest of those good young men were nowhere to be found. There was no support. I was broke, I was sick, I was tired and I was homeless and abandoned again. Bud, the older lifeguard, finally showed up one day with a bus ticket to Ohio.

He was involved with a porn ring and I was probably one of the targets. I hung out in his trailer off and on, and he had cameras everywhere. For some reason, he never asked me to strip for the photo op. He drove me and my one suitcase to the Greyhound station, made sure I was on board and waved as the bus pulled out towards the north, taking me to my very uncertain future. Bud saved me and my baby from a very dangerous shadow that day.

Days before, I had called my aunt in Ohio and told her I was coming home for a 'visit'. I made a point to let her know I had gotten married too. I managed to lift a gold ring from one of the party houses, put it on my finger, and hoped against all hope something magic would happen.

The trip back to Ohio was long and grueling. All I had were memories of the past and uncertainty of the future. I felt old and done. I was so frightened but had to hide it. After all, I was on the road with strangers, and by the look of my fellow passengers, these were shadow people, just like me. I can't remember a smile anywhere. Just sad faces heading north after some dream was crushed in the south.

Chapter Three

What Else Happened

How am I to negotiate with you if I don't know me?
If you love me you will find me somewhere in
your shadow.
Grace Spotted Eagle
Lakota Elder

Tap Dancing on Glass Tables, 1960 to 1970s
Historical and Social Highlights 1970s

US abandons gold standard and US dollar floats; Munich Olympics massacre; Watergate scandal; resignation of President Nixon; Soweto Uprising; decimalization of British currency; end of Vietnam War, Khmer Rouge killing fields; oil crisis; energy crisis; Jonestown mass deaths; Camp David Accords; IRA and the 'troubles' in Northern Ireland; Idi Amin; famine in Bangladesh; video games; microwave ovens; video cassette recorders; home computers; death of Janis Joplin and Jimi Hendrix; the Great Inflation; first mobile handheld telephones; US gas price rises from 40 cents a gallon in 1970 to 86 cents in 1979; Greenpeace born; women's rights; first email sent; world population hits four billion; Three Mile Island nuclear accident; Margaret Thatcher elected first woman British Prime Minister; voting age in US lowered to 18; smallpox eradicated; first 'test tube' baby born; Iranian Islamic revolution.

Tap dancing on glass tables seemed like a good idea at first. Something different, something exciting, kept me apart from people who dance on wooden floors. Being the center of attention was very important to me. As the dance got more intense, the pressure of feet on glass got more dangerous. Glass tables get weary of fools who dance there, until finally the fool breaks through, battered, bruised and cut from all that tap dancing. Then the GT sighs with relief until the next fool shows up. Alcoholic moms dance on glass tables often. They break through often. Addicted mothers have shredded feet and no one notices. Someone should notice.

The first time I got in touch with the reason I was trying to please everyone was my coming home to Ohio from Lauderdale. I remembered all the *Theys* I gave power to, who abused me, misunderstood me, ignored me, used me, and kept me in the Shadow Dance. Stepping up on a glass table with the shadow under me for once seemed like a good idea. My feet were bleeding and I needed the cold ground of frozen Ohio again. That's what happens when you dance on broken glass. Even glass has a shadow. The cold ground would feel good again.

Hello Tecumseh Road! Again

When I got back to Tecumseh Road I was alone, sick, branded a sinner, condemned, embarrassed, and all that. I would take a walk in my neighborhood and see neighbors peek out of their windows at me. I was entertainment. I was 19 years old. All I wanted was a mister of my own to love, a home of my own, some comfort and security, like I perceived they had. All I wanted was a good life. A good life eluded me and I did not know how to change that. All I knew was I was going to be entertainment for the neighbors for at least nine months.

Then There was Jeannie. Me a Mom?

Jeannie was born April 25, 1963. She is a miracle. I was given the choice to abort her. I chose not to take her life. I had no idea how to be a mom. It was brave of me to try. My mom wasn't around to model what that's about. My aunts certainly did not know, as they had no children. I had no friends who modeled mom-ism, or at least not the kind I wanted to be. I had the good fortune to have a friend who did know. Her name was June. She lived next door to us on Tecumseh Road.

The night I went into labor Aunt Mary drove me to the hospital and left me at the front desk to face the process of delivery alone. Mary was probably frightened beyond words, but still. The delivery was long, difficult, frightening and painful. Being alone makes things more difficult. There were too many people who had no idea what to do with me. Support is not what they chose to do.

June's husband was abusive but she held her own. She was from England. She met her husband while he was serving in Europe in the Air Force. She had five kids who became friends to my daughter. She helped me more than she knows. For one thing, I did not know I should not be drinking while pregnant. June alerted me and I stayed away from alcohol for nine months. I will always be grateful for June. She saved Jeannie's life and my sanity. Before I left Tecumseh Road she handed me a copy of the St Francis prayer. I carried that card in my wallet for many years.

Hard Work at Which Factory. First Marriage, Then?

When you have a child, are young (20 years old) and have no resources, you have to work at least two jobs to make ends meet. You work your ass off, knowing that you are it. You work out of guilt for the sinner you were branded to be. You work to the point of coma, lest you risk the little life you have. You work from fear of loss. Children are taken from you when you don't work hard. Single moms are compromised to the extreme. I worked at a factory putting motors together that would end up being electric fans, and at a local bar. I worked at a photo studio as a photographer. None of these jobs gave me enough money to support us. I had to find another way to support my child.

I found a man to marry in 1964. His name was Jim. He was at least 15 years older than I. He had diabetes, drank and gambled. But he was passive. Between us we could afford a condo in a decent part of Dayton, Ohio. That was the first legal marriage. I had sex with him maybe twice. We lived in the condo for about a year. He was an artist and worked for the Yellow Pages. He stayed home, watched Jeannie, and when I came home after two jobs I took over. I was numb all the time. The pills I chugged down helped keep me that way. One day I blacked out at the back screen door. Jim died in 1965 on our living room floor from too much of whatever too much was for him. He left nothing behind. I was alone again. I packed and left for Springfield, Ohio, back to Aunt Mary's again. She was totally nuts by this time. She obsessed over my child. She absorbed Jeannie. I was too weary to fight it.

Still Looking for Mister, 1965

I had to get away from Mary, the failure and her darkness. This Shadow overtook me, embraced me, hugged me, claimed me, and ate me alive. The Shadow was the only thing I had left. Thank God for those little white pills from Aunt Mary's vast supply, for whiskey, for beer, for wine, for vodka, for anything that kept me numb. Thank the gods of numb. I stayed in the zone for a long time. I lived in the deep bondage shadow of self. I maintained there. I looked like I was functioning to the others outside but I was in the land of the Shadow, my only country. I found mister, and off I went into another realm. I took me, my deep dark Shadow and my talent for falling from grace and dove over some unexplored cliff again. Oh well, been there, done that, and what's new?

Finding Rick in Ohio on My Way to Paradise, 1965–6

Rick was in the Air Force. He was handsome. A shit-kicking cowboy from Colorado. When I walked into that bar in Enon the world stood still (literally) and I fell in love immediately. I don't know if I was hallucinating or it was real, but when I walked through the swinging doors of the bar, the room froze, all sound stopped, and all I saw was Rick sitting at a table with his buddies, drinking his beer. It seemed a long time, but I realized I needed to meet this man. Betty, the gal I was with, who also had a kid out of wedlock, nudged me to go in, which broke the spell I found myself under. I led her to a table near Rick. Eventually, before the night was over, we met. We started to date.

Rick was attentive, careful, romantic, and made me feel special. I shared my lousy past with him and he understood. He had one of his own. He was kind. I had not felt kindness for a long time. I was starving for kindness. I was so hungry for handsome. I was hungry for normal, for love, for security, for a man I could claim as my own. And claim him I did. Drug addicts take hostages. It was not intentional, but there it was, as I found out later. Rick was also drinking and maintaining. The sex was really good. The hotels we hung out in on weekends, the buckets of Colonel Sanders chicken and TV and long talks way into the night were healing for me. I had my guy. We were as one.

Then one day he announced he'd got reassigned and

had to fly out of Ohio, headed to a base in Colorado or California or to the end of the world or to the moon, as far as I could understand. I could not lose Rick. I knew I had to make it work. The sacrifice was profound. Jeannie was only two years old.

Losing Jeannie and Impossible Choices, 1967

Are you a bad mother when you walk out the door on your way to the airport to fly out to meet the love of your life? Are you a bad mother when you look back and find your child curled up in a ball, crying her eyes out?

I made the choice to move to California with Rick. The idea was to go out, establish a home for Jeannie, come back and get her. Rick was just starting out as a new flight technician for the Federal Aviation Administration. He traveled non-stop. I hardly saw him, and when he did come home, we tried to reestablish connection, and then he was gone again.

I broke down every time he left. I was utterly alone in an apartment in LA. I tried to work, to attend art classes, to socialize with neighbors, but the mind-crushing loneliness and the drinking made much social life impossible. I was so frightened without Rick. I was totally dependent on him. Shadows named loneliness don't let go easily. They love patterns. Hello loneliness, my old pattern Shadow. Hello.

I missed my child. I was lost. I was paralyzed. I did not know how to get back to Jeannie. I had my first nervous breakdown.

A Doll Named Linda, 1970s

She was five years old when I finally got back. The courts in Ohio sent me an envelope, saying in it that I would have to fight for custody of my daughter. Aunt Mary contested me in court and claimed me an unfit mother. My long absence proved this to be true. The breakdown in my California apartment put Rick into white knight mode. He paid for a lawyer both in California and Ohio. This was a huge sacrifice. It was very expensive and took a toll on Rick's plans financially. I will be eternally grateful to him for his help.

We flew back to get my daughter. Oh my God, what a circus, what pressure, what drama, what a nail-biter this time was! Aunt Mary went totally sideways, she *kidnapped* Jeannie, took her hostage, hid her, so even though the court granted me custody, I still did not have her. Uncle Butch saw the insanity of this and told us where Jeannie was. We went to get her. She was a mess, we all were a mess, it was all a mess. What a horrible way to get reacquainted with my only daughter, who hated me. We packed this poor child up and took her back to California.

She hated me for a long time. Five thousand dollars later, Rick was broke. I think he must have resented me at this point but he did not show it. We moved to Aurora, Colorado, in 1973, bought a house and tried to be a couple with a child, but the drinking got worse for both of us. Jeannie was lonely, resentful and disconnected. Rick worked hard and drank hard. I zoned out hard and

Jeannie zombied back and forth to a local school. She lost her mom (me) and her doll, Linda, was her only comfort.

As with all life, I found things to do. Eventually, I joined the Aurora Chamber of Commerce, won an award, made some friends. The time in Colorado was not the happiest for us. Rick got a job promotion and was transferred to Los Angeles.

In 1974, while living in Torrance, California, I wrote for the *Daily Breeze* newspaper but couldn't keep consistency. As a drunk, it was hard to stay committed to the mundane job of daily writing. Drunks don't stay put. It's in the mind. My writing career went down the tube, just like I was doing little by little.

In 1978 I attempted to go to Pierce College and failed. There were many of these attempts to become successful and many failures. Simple things like making classes used to baffle me. No matter how hard I tried, I could not function. Alcoholism had me, owned me, drove me. That is the nature of this disease. It's important to understand this. This is a deadly Shadow Dance all addicts do. Only God Itself can break this darkness, and sometimes even that fails. Powerful is this 'ism'. Very.

Finally, Security on Zombar, 1980s
Historical and Social Highlights 1980s

Apartheid; Soviet war in Afghanistan; Iran-Iraq War; civil war in Lebanon; eruption of Mount St Helens; yuppies; AIDS; John Lennon murdered; marriage of Prince Charles and Lady Diana Spencer; MTV; boxer Muhammad Ali retires; space shuttle; Pope John Paul II shot; President

Ronald Reagan and Prime Minister Margaret Thatcher; Reagan shot; Falklands War; CNN; beginnings of the World Wide Web; Prime Minister of India Indira Gandhi assassinated; famine in Ethiopia and Sudan; Band Aid and Live Aid; global warming; discovery of a hole in the earth's ozone layer; Mikhail Gorbachev, perestroika and glasnost; Chernobyl accident; first Intifada; widespread use of crack cocaine; gas $1.19 a gallon; The Simpsons; Internet developed; Lockerbie air disaster; world population hits five billion; full independence of Canada, Australia, New Zealand, Zimbabwe; Tiananmen Square protests; fall of the Berlin wall; collapse of communism; end of the Cold War.

Rick had good work and good pay after many years of training. We were still young, bought a house in Van Nuys, California, on Zombar Street in a cul-de-sac, and started the good life in California. My neighbors were terrific. We partied a lot on that perfect street. We had friends across the street. Shelly, Sharon and Terry were very much a part of our lives. We were couples raising our only daughters, working, canning garden tomatoes, exchanging recipes, gossiping, enjoying many animals in large back yards, playing cards, eating pizza, and drinking on weekends.

Once in a while there were those funny little cigarettes but only once in a while. What fun! It was the first and only time I had a normal stress-free life. I even started to go to a local community school. I took art classes and found I was a good artist. I started to paint. Some of them sold. My favorite thing to do was to sit on a shelf meant for flower boxes outside my house, jack up Janis Joplin and drink my Wild Turkey whiskey. I was a beautiful woman. I had a decent voice. I had dreams and plans. I was one of the sunny people of California.

Many people came and went. Rick's friends were mostly fellow drinkers who watched football with him. Some were old friends (women) from Colorado he had been to school with who lived in California. We all became good friends. I thought the darkness of past days was at my back now. My face was turning to hope. Jeannie was in 4-H with prize French Lop rabbits.

I was a 4-H leader. We went to fairs and won blue ribbons. We had many prize animals. I met some wonderful people at this time in my life, like Betty and Joe Barns, who reminded mc of the Waltons. I was a young mother who was trying to make up for all the time I could not be a good mother. I made up with a vengeance.

Shadows Come Back with a Vengeance Too

But with all this positive activity, there were times of darkness. My drinking was getting worse. I had horrible incidents that were extremely troubling. I remember some Jehovah's Witnesses coming to the door to give me their good message. I was very angry that day and had been drinking hard. I opened the door and challenged them to prove there was a God. I asked them, 'Where was your God when I was being thrown down a flight of stairs when I was a kid?' They could not answer that question, so I pretty much insulted them and their God and threw them out of my home. They never came back.

Another incident that should have clued me in that I was out of control with my drinking was when I walked across the street with a rifle and threatened a family living there who, I was convinced, were abusing their kids. They probably were, as the kids would come to my house bruised. They did not call the police and moved out soon after.

Our lives were full of dune buggies, visiting our good drinking friends like Bill and Mary in Hermosa Beach, having friends over for parties, doing what young couples do at this stage of their lives. Bill was Rick's reloading buddy and they did this as a hobby for the ever-growing gun collection. Roaming around in our big Green Guy pick-up truck, having fun, was a regular practice.

There were many good times, but they started to become rare as the funny weed got stronger and laced, the parties got more dangerous, and the company got weirder. Rick's drinking got worse and he became deeply depressed. He was very unhappy. I was self-centered and too clueless to notice a lot that was going on around me. The most devastating was when my daughter was convinced Rick had targeted her in a dangerous way. I confronted him later on. He declared innocence. There are some shadows that tear holes into your very soul. This was one of them.

Our drinking and drugging started to bottom us out. We did not know this was what was happening, but we were both addicts. Rick drank many cases of Budweiser, and I was in love with anything strong and amber. Wild

Turkey whiskey and brandy for instance. I loved the way it burned going down, the way it warmed my body, the way it inspired my mind, the way it looked, smelled and felt as it permeated my body and numbed my mind. Whiskey – nectar of the Shadow gods. And this bottle – 'god of my understanding' – loved the way I loved it. I gave this small dark god all the power. I gave into the Shadow of addiction. It is 'cunning, baffling and power-ful'. Very!

Since I'm Out Here – I'm Out of Here . . . Part Two
June 1980

My story as written in my first book, *Needs*:

She sat silent in her mid 30s at a time of extreme conflict and made a choice that would change her life forever. She was in the process of negotiating her dramatic events, all the drama that accumulated over the years that led to this moment. On June 3rd, 1980, she was sitting at her living room table in Van Nuys, California, with a bottle of Wild Turkey whiskey, a line of cocaine, a loaded clip, the German Luger gun lying to her right. She sat half the night drinking; shot glass by shot glass, the amber whiskey sliding smoothly down her core, warming her cold heart, a ritual she had done for years. When she was done she snorted the line, slapped the clip into the Luger, put the barrel to her right temple and pulled the trigger. She was bottomed-out from her hard life. She was facing her death and jumped –

She was someone's daughter, she was someone's mom, she was someone's wife, she was someone's friend, she was someone's co-worker, she was part of the community and she was a citizen of the world. She was valuable and needed yet here she was – at a point of choice – and clearly she was making the wrong one. She was negotiating her shadows.[8]

Me

I need to know there is a place for me to land

A place to go to when I am finally bent and broken low

I need to know that the great messy slide out from some spot I landed in

from young to old will go well

I need to know that some remote God cares after all

That some laughing Buddha is not laughing at me

That some compassionate Jesus is resisting raising his eyebrows

That Moses went back to pick up that third tablet so we will know the rest of the story

That Mohammad would ride his magnificent steed towards me, hand out to pick me up

That Bahá'u'lláh really is Just

And that 'Abdu'l-Bahá is my grandfather,
the Master of love

Or are they all disappointed in me –

I need to know that I will not have lived in vain
that the empty canvas of me – embryonic –
was filled with striving acknowledged.

First Miracle: Shadow 0, God 1

My bottoming out was with a gun to my head. I passed out after pulling the trigger. The gun did not go off. I was too drunk and stoned to load the gun correctly. When I came to I realized what I had almost done and panicked. I went to the phone to call someone and saw a red emergency number under the phone. It was the AA hotline number that my daughter had gotten from an Al-Anon lady next door to us. I called that number and two women came from an Alano Club in the neighborhood to take me to an AA meeting. I was terrified. When I got to the meeting, I sat in the back of the room.

I was so sick, the two women sat with me. I did not hear a word anyone said. I looked up at the walls and saw the Twelve Steps of AA in individual pictures with the name 'God' in gold letters. I thought, 'Damn, this is a religion!' and I hated God and religion. I thought I was screwed and the only way out was to go home and finish the job. But these two women stayed with me for the night and took me to another meeting the next morning. It did not take too long to see that this AA was not a religion. It was sanctuary for drunks like me. I was assigned a sponsor, Susan, and went on to start my AA journey of sobriety.

Shadow to Sun, the Beginning of a Spiritual Awakening

My early sobriety was full of love. I had incredible support from AA, my sponsor Patty McN, even Rick and Jeannie. I went to a meeting every day. I was able to accumulate time, first chip-taking and then my first year of sobriety with a cake and cards. Celebrating sobriety with chips that mark sobriety time and cakes was/is typical of AA in California. Rick would come and watch me take a cake every year we were together during my first years in the program. Jeannie, Rick and I would go to AA Christmas dinners at the Alano Club. He did not get sober. He continued to drink.

I lived with Rick there in our house on Zombar for a few years into my sobriety. Eventually he moved out to live with his then gal pal, Jeannette. Perhaps it was stupid to prolong the marriage, perhaps it was risky, but because I worked a good strong program in AA, had a sponsor, sponsored other gals, did service work, I was safe. There were many attempts at exposing him to program. It was heartbreaking, losing him this way.

My Al-Anon sponsor, Lenney, and her husband, Cowboy Bill (in AA), befriended us. We went to many rodeos. Cowboy Bill was a professional bull rider. I just knew that Rick would embrace the program and ask Bill to be his sponsor. I had so much hope. Bill tried to show Rick how the AA program worked by being a good example. Being safe and trying to get someone into program can only happen for so long. It did not take for Rick. I had to move on and so did he.

To be able to stay sober/clean through this event was a miracle. That is the point I am trying to make in this book. AA is a miracle program. Without the help of the 'Great Mystery Power' I found in AA, I could not have gone through this kind of life event without losing myself. The program works.

This was my spiritual awakening. It was as if after many years a corked bottle blew its top and my spirit blew out into a world of light and magic. I found God is mysterious like that. I was surrounded with so much spirit from so many walks of life. I became a spiritual giant. My healing abilities came forth and I was able to help many people. When I consider where I came from, what my chances were of surviving all the abuse, the deep shadows that engulfed me, all of the past that was designed to snuff my spirit out, I have to be amazed and deeply grateful.

Adopted into the Tribe, 1983

Native American connection days happened when Wallace Black Elk, Grace Spotted Eagle, Don Perrot, Rolling Thunder and Hyemeyohsts Storm brought us sweat lodges for the backyard, and crystals, feathers, sacred pipes, where so many people did ceremony with drums. Finally I had a tribe I could identify with. Grace Spotted Eagle was a Lakota grandmother. She took me under her wing, taught me how to tie tobacco flags, how to conduct myself around sacred objects like the pipe, drums and sweat lodges. She was patient. She listened when I told her of my past. She had compassion. I told her how my people threw me away, how I longed for connection. I told her I wished I had been born into a family like hers, a family that cherished its young and had a grandmother like her. She said, 'Well, you do now.'

She adopted me in a sweat lodge ceremony. I was given a small crystal during this ceremony. I carried it with me all the time. It was my connection to my new family. Later on I was given a name by Don Perrot of the Potawatomi Winnebago tribes and Michael Noa, a Métis. My new name was Grace Growing Medicine. I was adopted into the Métis nation. The Métis nation is a tribe of people who are half this and half that. I found that I was a healer and dowser. This world opened to me through my adopted native family. I had the honor of hosting in my home many native leaders who traveled through Van Nuys as they came and went, working with the many lost people coming from divided backgrounds who were looking for community and connection. Being Métis gave me the identity that I so desperately needed. The crystal I took with me from the sweat lodge ceremony, loaded with prayers for addicted youth, became a gift to a goddess in Hawaii.

I started to blossom and gain confidence in myself, which gave me permission to explore my spiritual nature. In 1984 I flew with a group to an AA convention in Oahu, Hawaii. Magical things happened there. Someone had to cancel an island-hopping adventure and I was given the ticket to fly to all the islands. With that I was able to *meet* Pele, the fire goddess. I was told by the natives in the sweat lodge ceremony we had before the trip to find a way to give the crystal to Pele. I was simply going to take it to water edge, throw it in and ask it to find its way to the goddess. The ticket gave me the opportunity to give it to her more directly.

A native who understood my mission drove me to a path that led to a steam hole. I felt as if I was hearing Mother Earth breathing. I offered a prayer and tossed the crystal into the steam hole. The steam circled me. I know I had a deeply intimate, spiritual experience. It changed me. My spiritual journey got better and better as the magic unfolded itself and validated my path.

In 1985 I joined the La Crescenta Ashram outside Los Angeles where I met Swami Buddhanama who mentored me through the maze of spirituality from a Buddhist perspective. I started to teach metaphysics at a local university. I was sober for five years. Many people said they were inspired and were helped to find their own spiritual path. AA's Steps say to give it away as you find it. This helped assure my sobriety and allowed me to continue a spiritual awakening, as promised in the Twelve Steps.

Europe (the First Time): France, Germany and England, 1986-7

In 1986 one of those important things I so wanted to happen, happened and I took my first trip to Europe. While I was teaching metaphysics classes at the Learning Tree University, one of my students, Jenny, wanted to go to France. She spoke perfect French and I decided to go with her. My daughter stayed home to watch the animals and off we went. Before we left for Europe, we stopped by Echo Park, Pennsylvania, to visit Jenny's parents and family. Her father was a writer. It was good meeting them. Jenny was raised by two devout Catholic parents who loved her, supported her, educated her – all the things I missed – and yet she was an addict. She was in the process of bottoming out while on this trip. Her parents did not know what to do. Later on, after the trip, I was able to help them understand. I told them my story and they were able to get help for themselves through Al-Anon.

The trip over was wonderful and magical. We got two seats on a charter flight that had to fill all its seats in order to take off. We lucked out and got the seats for half of what it would have cost to fly to Paris. I had made some phone calls to some people I met who lived in Germany and they invited us there from Paris. In Germany, our friends knew some people in Glastonbury, England. The Glastonbury Festival was happening at the time. It was the first time I heard of the Bahá'í people and their Faith.

My Alcoholic Mind and Bahá'í

I was five years sober when I was exposed to the Bahá'í Faith. Some friends who were Bahá'í introduced me to this strange religion. I was not a religious person, so I was not looking for a religion to belong to. AA was enough. Step 3 suggests I have a 'God of my understanding', and the God of my understanding was '*I don't understand God*' (and, in fact, I was not sure I liked the Dude). My mantra when I was drinking was 'Where was this God when I was being beaten and thrown down flights of stairs as a child? Keep your damn God!' So I was not an easy sell when anyone came to me to tell me of a religion. So I let it go and figured that my friends would get weary of talking about it. They stopped, so I forgot about it.

Then something very mysterious happened after I returned to the States. Late one night in my bed, after I drifted off to sort of a half sleep, I had a vision of this man in a white turban and robes floating above me, pointing his finger at my heart. He had no face! It scared the heck out of me. It was like a ghost visiting me. I had been sober for seven years, so knew I was not drunk.

The next morning I called one of my friends, a Cherokee woman, Renee Pasarow (a Bahá'í who had had a near-death experience) and asked her about this vision. She asked me to come to her home. When I got there she showed me a picture of 'Abdu'l-Bahá, one of the central figures of the Bahá'í Faith. I realized I could not ignore this message and started to investigate the Faith. I became a Bahá'í in 1987.

I went on to teach classes at various universities. I had become educated in homeopathic medicine in Europe and was able to teach in the US. I trained to become a stress management facilitator. In 1988 I met another spiritual leader who used music to heal people. Fabien Maman and his Tama-Do helped me to understand the many forms of healing there were in the world. His music technique took another chunk of the shadow away.

I traveled to Mariposa, California, to teach classes, run medicine wheel and pipe ceremonies, and do healings, and the spirit was so alive in me. My marriage was unraveling all the time I was flying high and Rick continued to sink into his alcoholism.

1987. My daughter, Jeannie, graduated from Northridge University with honors. I was so proud of her. I battled my own alcoholic Shadow for so much of her life. I missed much of her growing up process. Alcoholism robs so much and it robbed me of being fully engaged with my daughter. We are OK today but I wonder what it could have been like. Too much was taken from us, all of us. That is the Shadow that has a life of its own and it reaches deep into lives of innocent people and destroys. Negotiating is all we have.

Losing Rick to the Shadow

Rick was born in Greeley, Colorado, to sharecroppers. His parents had nothing of their own. They were given a small house as hired hands of a large feedstock company. He was deeply embarrassed by his family origins. When I met Rick I had so many romantic dreams I wanted to come true for us. All I wanted was to settle down, shape a good married life with this man I truly loved, raise my daughter, and do what people do who have a good opportunity for security.

There were many things in those last days I did not know about him. He stayed remote and drunk while he was bottoming out. One day he flew out to Colorado, picked up his childhood 'sweetheart', Jeannette, a drunk, bottomed-out gal whose husband had just left. He brought her back to Van Nuys. I walked into my house, into my living room, after an AA meeting and there they were, sitting on my couch, very drunk. They announced they wanted to be together. Officially that is how my marriage ended. My first thought was to go out to the den, grab a gun and shoot them both. I called my sponsor instead. She told me, 'Get your butt over here.' This was my first big test of sanity after getting sober. I passed.

From that day I helped Rick and Jeannette move into their condo. I gave them the compassion and empathy I was told I needed to give suffering alcoholics. They were both in trouble with addiction. As I was turning more and more to sobriety, they were moving more and more towards their shadows of addiction. They eventually moved to Henderson, Nevada. At some point later on they both died from their disease. They both were given many chances to sober up. But they chose not to. Why some get sober and others don't, I don't know. It is a mystery left to science and the Great Mystery.

With every gain comes a loss. When your gain and loss are measured under the Shadow, it is profound on both ends. Losing Rick was a big loss in my life. Rick was symbolic of what could have been, what should have been. Losing Jeannie was also a big loss, but because of Rick, Jeannie was regained. So I guess I can speculate that there was some kind of trade-off deal happening in the Shadow world, and that it became evident to me when it was to be revealed. I wrote this poem years ago and it says a lot about this loss.

The Tip of His Hat

He's a cowboy

A real one

Bulls, boots, belts, booze, dogs, and pickup trucks

I married him

Married together 25 years

We rode off into the sunset together like Roy and Dale

Something I learned about cowboys

They tip their hats when something important is about to happen

It had been coming on for a while

Denial is easier than reality

One day, late mid-day, coolness coming into fall season, leaves just tipping yellow and green like they do when something important is about to happen

He called me, said he was coming over to get the rest of his gear

I said, ok

So there he stood in front of me

Good-byes are sometimes fatal to the soul

Love of my life said goodbye – after the hug – after the kiss – after the tears

He cried

*Cowboys don't often do that
Not manly*

Like dad taught it

He tipped his hat

His long, brown scarred, weather-worn fingers went to the tip of his Stetson

He had just put it on, you see, so he could exit, go, leave

Out the screen door, out the wooden door,

Onto the porch, down the porch stairs,

Leaving me alone

Something important was about to happen,
he tipped his hat

He looked at me with those steel blue eyes,
bloodshot from all the booze and sleepless nights
over at the hotel

He chose to live there, that last month, while he came
and went

Circling the main wagon, getting ready to
ride off into the sunset alone – this time Roy without his
Dale

There are events that change you

You know? Like dying and leaving and getting sick and
old

There are events that haunt you, go deep into the soul,
events that even God Himself can't fix

The last thing I remember is the back of his
broad shoulders in the suede jacket, the back of his boots,

*the back of his hat, leaving – exiting – going toward
the door*

So many years ago, still memories linger fresh

I long to see fronts of things coming at me,

toward me

I long for a tip of his hat

I long for important things to happen

Chapter Four

What It's Like Now

Relieve me of the bondage of self[9]
Historical and Social Highlights 1990s

Reunification of Germany; Hubble Space Telescope in orbit; Nelson Mandela released; Gulf War; Balkan wars after break-up of Yugoslavia; Soviet Union dissolved; Britain gives Hong Kong back to China; President George H. W. Bush; President Bill Clinton; economic boom; gas $1.34 a gallon; Rodney King and LA riots; 'mad cow' disease epidemic in Britain; European Union forms and Euro comes into being; Earth Summit, Rio de Janeiro; bombing of World Trade Center; Oslo Accords; Chechen wars; genocide in Rwanda; end of Apartheid; IRA agrees to a truce in Northern Ireland; Channel Tunnel under the English Channel opens; CD-ROM drive; 24-hour news cycle; O. J. Simpson murder trial; DNA identification of individuals; Oklahoma City bombing; 16 million Internet users by mid-decade, rising to 248 million users by 1999; new bird flu virus found; Congo wars; Taliban seize control in Afghanistan; Princess Diana dies; cloned sheep Dolly born; Global Positioning System (GPS) becomes fully *operational; construction starts on International Space Station; bombing of Omagh, Northern Ireland; discovery of dark matter and black holes in space confirmed; Google created; Columbine High School massacre; use of mobile phones becomes widespread; world population hits six billion.*

Negotiating Shadows and Finding Grace, 1990s

Turning my face to the Sun through the grace of the God I do business with, the Great Mystery Power that I found in AA was nothing short of a modern day miracle. When I bottomed-out that day in June 1980 from the Shadow Dance that was my life, I had two options: shoot my head off or join AA. Finding me again was difficult. There were so many conflicts around me, there was so much wreckage to clear up. I became my own shadow, the Grand Shadow of shadows. Bottoming out with a gun to your head because drugs and alcohol have become the 'go to' zone is pure insanity. Crawling out from under the blanket of insanity was a major deal. So I had to trust in the process before me. There were many, many angels around me. There were many events that steered me towards the security of the program and sanity. The longing for important things to happen, happened. The promises of AA came true. 'We are going to know a new freedom and a new happiness. We will not regret the past nor wish to shut the door on it.' Promises coming true.

Needs

I need to know that when the music stops

I won't

I need to know when there is no love to be found

I can still be found

I need to know that when I die, swallowed by the Mother, there will be a molecule or a cell left behind for redemption

So I can go on somewhere somehow

I need to make music and poetry and rhyme and verse to make some sense of all the insanity around/in/of me

I need to know the palm reader is real and some are not

I need to know that

The Need of Gods

I need to seek knowing

I need to know that curiosity will drive me to the cliff of understanding and not take me down those compelling steep rocky slopes

*I need to know I will not be punished because I want to
know stuff or speak it or dance it or screw it up*

I need to know how to get back

How to get back to you, God

You put me here and I don't know how to get back

What is it that You seek from me?

Seeking You, seeking me

*There is so much that mesmerizes me into illusions of
finding that which I seek*

*I seek you in the bottle and the smoke and haze of
brain and sound of metal that rocks*

I seek you in beds that roll and flesh that rots

So much suffering this search.

Haifa, Israel; Norway, Sweden, Finland, Russia 1990-1

It took a long time to choose to define my own path. I no
longer wanted or would allow my crazy family or past
to define me. Shadows love co-dependency. Transition
is not for the wimpy. It takes courage and faith. I had
the courage but was very weak on the faith part. I was a

new Baháʼí. I was somewhat new to AA. I was seeking my highest good. I was touching the light, and the shadows fled away. I was able to go on Baháʼí pilgrimage in 1991 and flew to Haifa, Israel. I flew out on June 4th, which was my 11 years sober/clean date. What a gift.

In 1992 over 30,000 people attended the Baháʼí World Congress in New York. I met Britt and Linda, two Baháʼís from Norway, and was invited to spend a year with them. I applied for a visa, updated my passport, and got my affairs in order to prepare for the trip. My dear friend Kathy Carter took my little dog Bear into her life so I could go. My heart ached for her and Bear. I knew I would miss them horribly, but knew I had to go too. I found that important events have to be acted on with courage and faith. I am glad for the 'it takes a village' that allowed me to leap into my destiny.

Do You Speak Steinkjar, Norway? 1993

Steinkjar is a small town in mid-Norway. The flight was long. I was sad to leave the US and excited about the journey ahead. Not understanding a word anyone was saying (until they switched to English) was isolating. I slowly learned Norwegian. I was hired as an ESL teacher, helping newly-arrived refugees from different countries of conflict. They were enemies in their own countries but in that little classroom, at the refugee center, we were one with each other, learning Norwegian. I was respected as their teacher. Experiences of oneness are rare anywhere. We were all grateful for the opportunity to demonstrate the power of respect and love.

The Sami people are fascinating people. A group of us traveled to the very far north of Norway to attend a Sami conference. They came from Sweden, Finland, Russia, even from the US. The Sami people were just forming their nation, defining their own flag and making a statement to the Norwegians and Swedes as to the status they wanted for themselves.[10]

The Sami were called Lapps before they defined, in their own language, who they were and what they wanted as a people. They were suppressed/oppressed by the government, assimilated into the Norwegian (and Swedish) culture by force. This movement was much like the continuing movement in the US for Native American nations. Many Native Americans came to that conference to share their experiences. To see the Sami and Lakota together, working out their mutual problems, was awesome. I got to meet Buffy Sainte-Marie and other popular figures and was part of the conference in many ways.

Leaving Östersund, Sweden, 1997

I spent five years in Europe as a pioneer, healer, teacher, friend and traveler. Considering where I came from, those magic years in Europe were living, breathing, working miracles. The age of miracles is still with us and it is nice to know. Miracles drive shadows away. My dear friends Margareta Osterberg and her husband Goran embraced me, drove me around to places that are special to Sweden, including a 'magic' tree that the ancient healers used to heal babies of rickets in her home village.

Margareta spent her summers in her family's

traditional cow house. The young women were given the task of attending the cows and goats up pasture, where they flirted with the young men and bonded with friends. She had many stories of these times under the Swedish summer sky.

The Swedish culture, her childhood experiences, were so different from my childhood and yet here we were sitting together over coffee, chatting about the magic of the day. Marga and I are in close touch. Her husband Goran just passed while this book was being edited. I miss you, dear friends. I am blessed to have you in my life, Marga. Someday, if the gods allow, we will sit in the cow house and chat over coffee again.

Northern Lights, Moose and Alaska

Alaska is a magical place with the northern lights, the moose, the geese that gather and land at Creamer's Field, a wildlife refuge in the middle of Fairbanks. The summers are short but powerful. The light never leaves. The sun lingers on the horizon before it pops up again to warm the earth. When the fair came to town in August, we knew the summer was just about over. The sun started to sink below the horizon and soon enough the first snow came, as did the ice. Time to plug the car in again, time to put the snow tires on, time to get the ice grips for fur-lined boots and the goose down jacket out of the closet and get ready for a long dark winter. Ritual of the far north.

Even though it was dark and cold, it was very manageable. Northern lights and warm, lit shops where people gather and bunch up negate dark and cold somehow. It is an instinct to gather where there is light, something I took for granted before Alaska.

I had to leave my precious Alaska. I had to say goodbye to my friends, the moose and eagles and geese and the magical northern lights. I have multiple sclerosis, which got worse, and I realized it would be almost impossible to navigate in 20 below zero in a wheelchair. I still grieve the parting of me and Alaska.

The Shadow as Healer in Degrees, 2010
Historical and Social Highlights 2000s

Second Intifada; President George W Bush; International Space Station; Wikipedia launched; music downloads increase in popularity; gas $1.61; terrorist attacks on American targets by al-Qaeda 9/11; War on Terrorism declared; first artificial heart transplant, Lord of the Rings films; International Criminal Court established; end of Sierra Leone civil war; Guantanamo Bay detention camp; SARS near pandemic; Iraq War; Space Shuttle Columbia disintegrates during re-entry; last flight of Concorde; Human Genome Project completed; Harry Potter; an old human species, Homo floresiensis, discovered; Saddam Hussein captured; war in Dafur; gas $2.10; 9.3 magnitude earthquake in the Indian Ocean triggers massive tsunami; terrorist attacks in Madrid, London and Mumbai; Facebook launched; Hurricane Katrina; gas $3.18; Pope John Paul II dies; Iran's nuclear program starts; Saddam Hussein executed; hijacking of ships by Somali pirates; Mexican drug war; coup in Thailand; Michelle Bachelet elected first female President of Chile; Pluto is demoted to

*a 'dwarf planet'; former Pakistani Prime Minister Benazir
Bhutto assassinated; collapse of Lehman Brothers; Fidel
Castro steps down; banks fail; imprisonment of Bahá'í
leaders in Iran; first African-American President elected,
Barack Obama; Burma cyclone; CERN's Large Hadron
Collider completed; swine flu pandemic (H1N1 virus);
Michael Jackson dies; Tea Party movement.*

Conflict in Conflict Resolution

Our education system is broken. My firsthand experience, proving my statement is valid, is embedded in
the following story. After coming down from Alaska
where I received a BA in Drama Therapy from UAF
(University Alaska Fairbanks), I was accepted into the
Conflict Resolution Master's program at a university in
Oregon. The Conflict Resolution department was hell-
bent on encouraging older women of my type to fail. This
is my opinion, but when I talked to other older women,
I realized it was truth. Why a university would allow
professors to engage in this kind of sabotage is beyond
me. I went to the Dean of the College of Liberal Arts to
'complain' about the lack of support from my professors
and in essence nothing was done. I learned that this was
a world unto itself, full of very conflicted, fearful, ego-
centered people trying to hold onto whatever security
they thought they had. Whatever the problem, it affects
students with profound stress and conflict. It would
be comical to have this much conflict in the Conflict
Resolution department if it weren't real. Students don't
need to run this gauntlet. Borrowing money to get a

degree is a challenge unto itself. Added stress designed to eliminate certain students is unforgivable. It happens across the US every day and has to change.

I graduated with a 3.85 grade point average and would have gotten a 4.0 had it not been for one of those professors who took issue with a paper I had written that did not satisfy her impossible specifications. As a professional transformative mediator, I know there is nothing left but transformation and transition after the trip of denial, experimentation, struggle, victory and defeat and all the stuff that life is about. Considering how I struggled to get a degree while a drunk, getting a Master's degree was a *major victory*, won in spite of the atmosphere. The Sun won this one.

This Life 101 trip is scary, fascinating, infuriating and mysterious all at the same time. It is hard to be a human being. But since I am a human being, I have to find a way to be authentically human and accept all my flaws, character defects, potential and, most of all, I must treat myself and you with great empathy and compassion, honoring all the suffering it takes to be a human. I must celebrate my victories and yours. I must stay curious and fascinated. I must keep moving forward into the light. I choose to die in peace, no matter how much chaos is around me. I must, or I will not have been true to myself and the ancestors who struggled their way through the dark and messy shadows on their way to the Sun.

Chapter Five

Understanding the Shadow Dance

The past is a foreign country;
they do things differently there.
L. P. Hartley

Historical and Social Highlights 2010s – So Far

Global financial crisis; sovereign debt crisis in Europe; Deepwater Horizon oil spill; tallest building in the world, Burj Khalifa in Dubai, opens; Wikileaks; earthquake in Haiti; megathrust earthquake in Chile probably shifts Earth's axis; Pakistan floods; volcanic events at Eyjafjallajökull in Iceland ground millions of passengers; Copiapó, Chile, mining accident; Avatar is first film to cross the billion mark in the worldwide box office; UN Women established with Michelle Bachelet as head; attempted assassination of US Congresswoman Gabrielle Giffords; Japanese earthquake causes a tsunami that severely damages nuclear power plants; South Sudan created; Osama bin Laden killed; Kathryn Bigelow

*first woman to receive Academy Award for Best Director;
Libyan civil war; Arab spring; Colonel Muammar Gaddafi
killed; Iraq War officially over; young people massacred
in Norway; deadly tornado outbreak hits United States;
gas costs $3.43; Occupy movement; world population
hits seven billion.*

Face the Sun

*I was born with my back to the Sun. My parents were born
with their backs to the Sun. Their parents were born with
their backs to the Sun. When will we face the Sun? The
question remained and it finally dawned on me that when
I have my back to the Sun I will see my Shadow there on
the ground, stretched out in shades of gray. As I move,
it moves. I follow my Shadow and it is my leader. 'Turn
around', they said. I faced the Sun but the Shadow was still
there behind me. But I am its leader now. It took courage to
turn my face to the Sunlight of the Spirit. The generations
clapped and sighed. 'Finally! Freedom!' they said.*

The Anarchist with a Design for Living, 2010–11

At this writing I am in my thirty-first year of sobriety. If
you have read to this page, you have followed one addict's
journey from deep conflict (Shadow) to a spiritual awakening (Sun). My past was hard, rocky and long. I spent
most of my youth in the shadows of my insecurity, loss,
addiction and uncertainty. I learned how to be a rebel, an
anarchist. Today I try to help others find their path out
of the Shadow Dance. My life's focus is service to others.
But this is not easy. As I stated at the beginning of this

story, the Shadow is still there. It is behind me. All I have to do is turn my face away from the 'Sunlight of the Spirit' and the dark Shadow will lead me right back to the gates of hell. This is the legacy of an addict. Many addicts turn back to their shadows to be devoured by the dark. That is the purpose of this book, the reason I share my journey. I have witnessed how powerful the conflicts are for my fellow addicts and how many are lost to this disease.

The past can and does cast a long shadow for most addicts. But long shadows occur when the Sun is low on the horizon. Knowing the nature of this kind of shadow is important for the addict. Clearing up the anger and resentment of the past, the wreckage, is essential if the Sun of Spirit is to shine forth. The purpose of maintaining spiritual awakening and staying in a place of service to others is so it can be given away. The endgame of Step 12 of AA is staying spiritually awake and giving what you have found to the next suffering alcoholic/addict. People who work the program are spiritual giants!

The History of AA
When Spirit Landed on a Drunk

Bill W. (Wilson) was a bottomed-out, dying, chronic drunk. Dr William D. Silkworth worked in a hospital in New York that specialized in treating alcoholism. He worked endlessly with hopeless, desperate alcoholics and their families with little success until in 1934 he witnessed a modern-day miracle when Bill had a spiritual experience in the hospital. As he lay dying in his hospital bed, Bill saw a 'white light'.[11] From this experience, AA was born, from Spirit. Dr Silkworth said, 'We doctors have realized for a long time that some form of moral psychology was of urgent importance to alcoholics, but its application presented difficulties beyond our conception.'[12] The application of synthetic knowledge did not move the alcoholic to sobriety until a Power greater than himself pulled him back from the gates of death. That Power (Sun) took me by the nape of my neck and yanked me back to terra firma, away from illusions of personal power and into the majestic reality of Life 101. All I have to do is stay put, stay where I find myself planted and work the program.

The World Needs an AA Meeting

AAs speak the language of the heart in all its power and simplicity.[13]

When I was doing research for my Master's thesis I ran across a book called *When Society Becomes an Addict* by Anne Wilson Schaef (1987). In her book Schaef describes society, especially at corporate level, around the banking and justice systems, as acting as an active addict behaves. An active addict is selfish, self-centered, resentful, angry, dishonest, pathological, etc. Public, social, political, educational and religious systems parallel personal addictive pathological behavior, according to Schaef. Nothing much has changed today from the influences on my parents in the 1920s. We need a new model of behavior in individuals and societal lives. The world needs an AA meeting.

In meetings I learned that I had never known how to live life. I muddled through from day to day, event to event, through periods of luck and loss. I did not feel in control of my fate, my choices, my thoughts or my path until I fell into AA and was exposed to and taught spiritual principles. My parents, my schools, my social systems, the justice system, even religious organizations could not teach me this path. I was truly on my own. This is the state of many youth, even though we are living in the 21st century. The news is filled with drug problems, family violence, compulsive, driven politics and failed justice systems. The human family needs a break.

As a really messed up rebel used to doing things my own way no matter what, it was like falling onto a soft pillow from a pile of hard rocks when I got into AA. The Bahá'í Faith added detail to my spiritual awakening. In AA people loved me no matter what. They cared if I lived or died. They asked me to follow a simple path that would lead to freedom. This was real. This is what I had been looking for all my life. I finally came home when I got into AA in 1980. For me to find AA, or for AA to find me, was a living miracle.

I have the family I was robbed of as a child. Over the years I've sponsored many people, including gays, lesbians and trans identified. It does not matter what the color, sexual orientation, culture or any of that. All that matters is the service I can offer another suffering addict. I go to at least three meetings a week, sponsor several women, have a sponsor who became sober in 1970 and do service work. The deep dark Shadows that followed me most of my life don't exist today as long as I stay sober/clean.

Why can't the world do this too? We need to change. I hope this book motivates investigation towards that end.

Communicate Already

I live in two worlds. One is rife with depression, suicide, addiction, gang violence, a 75 per cent recidivism of our youth, and many other severe conflicts and problems. I live in a world in the year 2011 that still does not communicate non-violently, that chooses apathy as a response to the tragic events in front of its eyes. I live in a world that jails its addicts, continues to ignore its homeless population, marginalizes its oppressed elders, struggles with its deeply divided partisan politics, saves its banks and car industry and refuses to prioritize housing for those dumped out on the streets due to foreclosure. I live here where oil spills and global warming take their toll, where wildlife and the environment are falling apart. I live in a world where religion is insane. Sweet hearts, minds and souls are broken, as poverty in the US gets deeper.

What is so different in my world in 2011 from the one I was born into in 1943? What is so different from when my parents were born in the 1920s? Systems are still broken and the dilemmas deepen worldwide. The thing that is different is the World Wide Web that records our doings every day. This tool gives us perspective and the responsibility to grow up. It's all in our face. The present Occupy Wall Street movement is attempting to address all of this. Perhaps over time its promoters will be understood and supported.

There is a solution. We need to get back to spiritually-based thinking and doing. We need to get in touch with our spirit and connect to Universal Truth, whatever that is. We need unity and love. We need renewal, and now! There is no place left to go but to the peace circles where all people are at one with each other and truly care for each other in spite of our propensity to divide and conquer. The ancients weren't wrong.

Bahá'í is a Hard Sell but, Then, It Does Not Sell

The Pew study on religious knowledge[14] revealed something about American society that Professor David S. Gutterman of the political science department of Willamette University, Oregon, pondered when visiting my university: 'It raises an interesting question: whether or not ignorance about our own religion or other religions is the source of religious divisiveness in the United States. I think that answer is no. You can know a whole lot about somebody and still think that they're fundamentally wrong. To me the problem is not ignorance – it's arrogance.'

I don't know why some things are so hard to explain. When I hated 'God' there was no way I could be open to receive any message except the one in my own head. Since I was insane at the time, the only message was an insane one. I survived the severity of my life. It's good for my soul to share what I found, especially if the message motivates change.

The Bahá'í Faith promises me a renewal of all life on Planet Earth like no other renewal known to mankind so far. It tells me that I am one with all other people, that I am part of a progressive revelation. Check it out for yourself. I see it as a way to heal the human race on many levels (www.bahai.org).

I never thought I would promote this kind of message. I hate preaching, but I look around and see we as a people are falling apart. I see Mother Earth violated at every level. Where else are we to go? I opened my alcoholic mind and embraced the God of my understanding (the Great Mystery), and while I am not the best Bahá'í I can be, I do my best to follow the dictates of my conscience.

The Big Book of AA tells me how to live life free of the insanity of drinking/drug use, which is a pretty good deal for an anarchist and rebel. I owe much to the Bahá'í Faith. Some of the best years of my life were when I was traveling throughout northern Europe as a pioneer sharing the Hopi prophecy that mentions the Bahani (Bahá'í) as being a renewed religion for this time. The human race is one race and the Earth is sick of us and our immaturity and violence! We have an opportunity to achieve a whole family system of recovery for all people, whether physically addicted to some substance or not.

What It's Like Today
Grace Writes for Portland Addiction Examiner.com, 2010

According to the police of Portland, alcohol and drug addiction is a main factor in the calls they go out to negotiate. The police are more social worker than cop and it is crazy and very dangerous for all involved. I have been writing for examiner.com for a few months about addiction issues and the impact they are having on our community. National statistics show that just about every community in the nation is affected by drug/alcohol problems.

We, as a nation, choose to hang onto our guns and alcohol, which produces a lot of violence in people already stressed to the max. We are a new nation (only 200 years plus), still in the stage of working it out, working our way to the seasoned antiquity of other nations. There is much to do as we advance our systems towards maturity. At the time of writing, the 'Drug Free Zone' concept is back on the table. City government is trying to legislate addiction, pushing the problem from one community to another, which will not work. As never before, there is need for treatment centers, for more education about addiction in the schools, prisons, in the community and in the home.[15]

Broadcaster for kboo.fm radio

We are coming up on the year 2012 in a month. I think back on my grandparents' time in the 1920s, how their lives were, what they were doing, how they were living, how they negotiated their shadows and enjoyed their sunshine days. I think of all the times my parents were living their lives as best they could in a world that stubbornly hung onto past habits of conflict, war, greed and pride, but always with some hope that the future would bring more peace and security. My childhood was not better in spite of their efforts. Many children today are

living in less than the best society could choose to provide. Many do turn towards drugs/alcohol and violence.
Many are in prison as a result. All we can do is share our
experience, strength and hope with those who are negotiating their shadows on the way to the Sun.[16]

Published Book, Needs, 2009

Needs is dedicated to the homeless youth who vote with
their feet, to days we spent at Guerilla Theater developing the script 'Children of the Other Shoe' and to the
addicted youth of Residential Alcohol/Drug (RAD)
Community Justice Juvenile Services Department, the
staff and their outside helpers. Their severe life struggles
inspired creativity and allowed space for an open-ended
process to happen. We came together in a state of hard-
earned trust and talked from the heart on those magic
days in Portland, Oregon, as the process unfolded on our
journey to the Sun of our spirits.

The poems and short stories in the book reflect the life
experiences of addicted youth at risk who were unsuc-
cessful in their communities and were placed in juvenile
justice. Life is especially hard for addicted at-risk youth
who have failed past treatment. The RAD unit was their
last chance for better choices. The youth who wrote their
poems were aged between 13 and 17 and influenced my
own poems reflecting societal attitudes, the need for
understanding, and the struggle to understand what
needs to change.

We are losing youth to drugs at an alarming rate.
We need a new way of dealing with this loss. Economic

changes, use of non-violent communication, revamped educational and juvenile justice systems are essential.

The need for restorative and transformative models of justice, such as the RAD unit, is evident. This book is dedicated to that effort. The poems will become lighter as the light of true justice shines on the youth of RAD and all like them. May the grace of fairness find us all on our journey to compassionate and restorative justice.

The Fire of Street Joan: A Documentary, 2011

I met Elizabeth Weissenborn at a meeting of the Northwest Film Institute's Sisters in Cinema. I went there to beg for a documentarist to help me film the situation on Portland's streets, with their homeless, mentally ill, marginalized women and at-risk youth. I had bought a small handheld camcorder and tried to do the documentary myself but I ride around on a scooter and could not pull it off. So I ended up over at NFI with a plea for help. Well, what a blessing Elizabeth was. She came over and put her card down. We met and started to plan the documentary. Our film will be out in 2012. This poem started the whole project.

The Fire of Street Joan[17]

Tortured by Fire   That strange heat

Burning away passion   Of the day

Ordered by the   Trend of the Age

Political correctness

Clashing with That Church

White hided hoofed runner

Ushering her to the wood pyre

Look how she burns

For the good of us all

Her fire need

Our need of fire

Whole System Recovery

At this writing we are heading towards a 'whole system recovery', a term coined by Anne Wilson Schaef. Our society has been acting like an addict for the 200 years it's been in existence. People are bottoming out, coming too/to and growing up. As the Sun gets stronger and the shadows get weaker, future generations will have it better.

My Wish for All Addicts

May all your shadows fly away.

May you find joy.
May peace be yours.

May we all find a way to make this Earth heavenly.

Where we can live in freedom and joy

'as you trudge the Road of Happy Destiny'.[18]

The Shadow Poem

Letter to a Friend

I salute you! . . . There is nothing I can give you which you have not got.
But there is much, very much, that while I cannot give it, you can take.
No heaven can come to us unless our hearts find rest in it today. Take heaven! No peace lies in the future, which is not hidden in this present instance.
Take peace. The gloom of the world is but a shadow. Behind it, yet within our reach, is joy. Take joy! . . .
And so I greet you, with profound esteem and with the prayer
that for you, now and forever, the day breaks and the shadows flee away.

Fra Giovanni, 1513

Notes and References

1. National Survey on Drug Use and Health. Substance Abuse and Mental Health Services Administration (SAMHSA): http://idpc.net/publications/2010-national-survey-on-drug-use-and-health-in-the-usa
2. National Institute on Drug Abuse. http://www./drugabuse.gov/publications/infofacts/drug-related-hospital-emergency-room-visits
3. ibid. Table 14.
4. Treatment Episodes Data Sets (TEDS) 1999–2009. National Admissions to Substance Abuse Treatment Services. Department of Health and Human Services. Substance Abuse and Health Services Administration (SAMHSA). Rockville, Maryland, April 2011. http://wwwdasis.samhsa.gov/teds09/teds2k9nweb.pdf?
5. Alcoholics Anonymous, *Big Book*, chapter 5, 'How It Works'. http://www.aa.org/bigbookonline/
6. Website of Alcoholics Anonymous. http://www.aa.org/subpage.cfm?page=1
7. Alcoholics Anonymous, *Big Book*, pp. 83-4.
8. E.R., Grace Growing Medicine. *Needs*, Introduction. Self-published, 2009. http://www.negotiatingshadows.com/pages/books.html
9. Alcoholics Anonymous, *Big Book*, p. 63.
10. See my book *The Sami Connection*.
11. 3rd step prayer, in Alcoholics Anonymous, *Big Book*, p. 1.
12. ibid. p. xxvii.
13. ibid. p. xxiv.
14. Pew Forum on Religion and Public Life, 'U.S. Religious Knowledge Survey', September 28, 2010. http://pewresearch.org/pubs/1745/erica-survey-atheists-agnostics-score-highest
15. http://www.examiner.com/addiction-in-portland/grace-e-reed
16. Mondays 6:30/7 p.m. http://kboo.fm/PrisonPipeline
17. E.R., *Needs*, p. 26.
18. Alcoholics Anonymous, *Big Book*, p. 164.

www.ingramcontent.com/pod-product-compliance
Lightning Source LLC
Chambersburg PA
CBHW030027290326
41934CB00005B/515